Breakthrough Therapy Techniques for Individuals, Groups, Kids and Adults

A Cookbook of Activities

Amber Ferraez Kuntz

iUniverse, Inc.
New York   Bloomington

Breakthrough Therapy Techniques for Individuals, Groups, Kids and Adults
A Cookbook of Activities

iUniverse books may be ordered through booksellers or by contacting:

iUniverse
1663 Liberty Drive
Bloomington, IN 47403
www.iuniverse.com
1-800-Authors (1-800-288-4677)

Because of the dynamic nature of the Internet, any Web addresses or links contained in this book may have changed since publication and may no longer be valid. The views expressed in this work are solely those of the author and do not necessarily reflect the views of the publisher, and the publisher hereby disclaims any responsibility for them.

ISBN: 978-1-4401-3863-8 (pbk)
ISBN: 978-1-4401-3864-5 (ebk)

Printed in the United States of America

iUniverse rev. date: 4/24/09

ACKNOWLEDGEMENTS

I am so thankful to the many people that helped piece this book together: Paula DiBonaventura, Caitlan Ferraez, Jade Ferraez, Jennifer Silva, and Christie Stockstill, who edited and aided in the creativity of the names and games. I am grateful for the opportunities at the facilities, schools, and with the numerous professionals and clients who gave this book more reason to come to life. I must acknowledge Mississippi State University and the many professors who taught me. Last, I give a special thank you to my parents, my husband, Johnny, and child, Adison who were so patient while I was working on this book.

About the Author:

Mrs. Amber Kuntz is a licensed professional Counselor and a Nationally Certified Counselor. She is a family and child outreach therapist who sees clients in the convenience of their own homes, in office, or in relaxed environments. She is a clinical/professional member of ACA. She speaks at workshops nationally and has published numerous journal articles. She most recently launched the Bright Future Mentor and Tutoring Program. www.ambercounselor. com

Contents

OUTLOOK OF ACTIVITIES

	Indiv.	Couples	School	Sibling	Family	Group	Ice Breaker	Team Work	Communication	Self-Esteem	Social Skills	Feelings
Tower Talk	X	X	X	X	X	X	X		X			X
Tower Assessment	X	X	X	X	X		X		X			X
How I Role	X	X		X								
Chit Chat	X	X		X								
Let's Connect	X	X	X	X			X			X		
What I Like	X		X	X		X		X				
Special Me	X	X		X	X	X						
Face your Feelings	X											X
Finders Keepers	X		X	X								X
Piece Together	X								X			X
Hunt	X			X	X				X			
Fun and Find	X			X		X					X	
Good or Not	X	X		X								X
I Can					X	X				X		X
Group Hoop				X	X	X		X	X			X
Walk this Way	X			X		X		X	X			X
Guess What			X	X	X	X	X		X			X
Meet in Middle				X	X		X					X
Pyramid	X		X	X		X		X	X			X
One log			X			X		X	X			X
Grow Away Habits	X			X	X	X						X
Marbles	X	X		X	X	X			X	X	X	
Grow Away Grief	X	X	X	X	X	X			X			X

INTRODUCTION

You are a first year teacher or school counselor, and you want to build self-esteem, friendships, and a bully-free atmosphere.

You just went though a divorce and do not know how to approach talking to your child about his or her feelings.

While on your family computer you find conversations between your fourteen-year-old and her friends about her sexual experience.

Your six-year-old daughter complains of her roommate/brother waking her up in the middle of the night. What's going on?

You have been married for twenty-five years and feel like you live with a roommate instead of a husband. You wish you could understand each other's feelings more and communicate better.

This book is for you.

While each of these examples deals with a different scenario, they all have one thing in common: a person in need of sensitive, non-judgmental support as he or she tries to reach people important to them. This book is filled with breakthrough techniques and fun hands on approaches that work for people of all ages.

ABOUT THIS BOOK //

If you are looking for a way to reconnect with your children, students, team, spouse, or elderly parent, this book is for you. *Breakthrough Therapy Techniques for Individuals, Groups, Kids, and Adults* is a collection of therapeutic activities for every day people, as well as professionals. I have taken familiar toys and games and transformed them into therapeutic interventions. Activities include ice-breakers and getting-to-know-you exercises, in addition to various activities meant to address issues such as grief and loss, anger, self-esteem, divorce, and much more.

This book is meant to offer help for individual, sibling, couple and group challenges. All activities can be altered to fit the client and atmosphere. These activities have been proven effective in such disciplines as social work, child and youth counseling psychology, correctional services, parent coaching, family or sibling counseling, and group work. Though this book is easy to understand and made for the common parent who needs approaches that kids will love, and their partner will too, the activities can also be used in settings such as mental health centers, hospitals, child welfare agencies, and schools.

Persons using this book need to be cautious of how material is conveyed. Participants' responses are not to be translated or manipulated. If further concerns arise, seek a Licensed Support System.

The activities in this book have been divided into four sections. The activities and themes cover such topics as: abuse, sibling rivalry, academic problems, family dynamics, anxiety, depression, friendships (or lack of) and other important topics.

Each activity is first described and discussed. Materials needed to complete an activity are outlined. The resource section at the back of the book details where particular materials may be obtained. Several of the activities include worksheets that can be copied and reproduced. The book includes detailed instructions for all activities.

While a description is given for each activity, any activity can be adapted for various clients and situations. On the provided worksheets there are some blank slots left for adding extra, or adapted, material. Flexibility and creativity is encouraged to suit the particular client, family, or situation.

Some activities may appear to be more suitable for a specific age range. This is not necessarily true. Parents are surprised what they learn about their own children or even their spouse when playing games. The elderly also like to play games. As long as you are using this book in the best interest of the person you are trying to help, and modify it for their age, it will work for basically any age.

SECTION ONE:

Ice Breakers
Getting to Know You
Assessments

TOWER TALK
Theme: Ice Breaker and Getting To Know You

Materials:
*Stacking Block Game such as Jenga

Advance Preparation:
None

Description and Discussion:
Begin by asking the client if they have ever played the game Jenga. For those who are unfamiliar with the game, quickly go over the rules, and for those who do know it, tell them that you will play a varied version, described as follows.

Decide who will go first, or ask the client if they would like to go first. This will tell you how comfortable they feel.

To set up the tower, place three blocks facing down. On top of the initial three blocks, add three more blocks crossways. Keep on stacking blocks, three one way, then three across those, until there are no more blocks.

To begin, pull out a block. (Some place the blocks back on top while others keep the blocks. It does not matter which way you play the game.) As the person takes a block out he or she tells something about him or herself or asks a question. Start off saying basic things like, "I have a dog," or "I love chocolate ice cream." Some clients tell more in depth things right away, while others just tell every day getting to know you things. You stop playing the game when the blocks fall. If the blocks fall too quickly you can chose to start over.

***It can be effective to play this game again around the third session. The client wants to try harder to keep it from falling for one and two you know some basic things about them so it can be used now to get to know more in depth information. As the clinician, you can encourage clients to be more open by telling things about yourself on the same topic.

Since most people find the game Jenga enjoyable, they should find this version engaging and relatively non-threatening. During the game there are ample opportunities to gather information, ask further questions, and build the counseling relationship or whatever relationship you are trying to encourage.

Modality:
Tower Talk is best used in individual or group therapy when getting to know clients for the first time. This game can be used in a school, agency, hospital or private setting. The game is also helpful when used at home between parents and their children or between siblings. Nursing homes have used this technique as a getting to know you activity to break the ice in a fun, light hearted way.

Individual
School
Couples
Sibling
Family

Jenga is a trademark of Hasbro. All rights reserved. Used with permission.

TOWER TALK (alternate version)
Theme: Assessment

Materials:
*Stacking block game such as Jenga

Advance Preparation:
Copy each question from the Jenga Assessment question card page, cut them apart and put them into a bowl. It is helpful to copy questions on card stock and laminate if you plan on reusing.

Description and Discussion:
Begin by asking the client if they have ever played the game Jenga. For those who are unfamiliar with the game, quickly go over the rules, and for those who do know it, tell them that you will play a different version, described as follows.

Decide who will go first, or ask the client if they would like to go first. This will tell you how comfortable they feel.

To set up the tower, place three blocks facing down. On top of the initial three blocks, add three more blocks crossways. Keep on stacking blocks, three one way, then three across those, until there are no more blocks.

To begin, pull out a block. (Some place the blocks back on top while others keep the blocks. It does not matter which way you play the game.) As the blocks are removed a question is pulled at random from the pile of chosen questions. Jenga assessment is effective, especially if used after playing Tower Talk since players feel like they are playing the game differently and being challenged more. They are also curious as to what is on the colorful question cards.

Modality:
Tower Talk can be used in any private, comfortable setting. Any practitioner, professional, or concerned person with the appropriate intent can use these approaches.

Individual
School
Couples
Sibling
Family
Ice Breaker
Assessment
Communication
Friendship

Jenga is a trademark of Hasbro. All rights reserved. Used with permission.

BASIC ASSESSMENT QUESTIONS

If you could change one thing about yourself, what would it be?	If you could change one thing about your family, what would it be?
What makes you happy?	Who do you consider your closest friends, and what do you like to do with them?
What do you think about the most?	Do you ever worry?
Do you have dreams? Do you have nightmares?	Tell me about a problem you are having.
Tell me about a time you did something fun.	Tell me about a time at school.

SIBLING ASSESSMENT QUESTIONS

What is your favorite memory with your sibling?	What would you like to change about your relationship with your sibling?
What do you fight about the most?	What is your favorite thing to do with your sibling?
EXTRA:	If your sibling changed one thing about you what would they change?
What do you frequently laugh about when you are together?	Tell me a time you felt happy when you were with your sibling.
Tell me a time you felt sad or angry.	Tell me a special memory of you and your sibling.

HOW I ROLE
Theme: Ice Breaker

Materials:
*Toilet paper

Advance Preparation:
None

Description:
Tell group or client to take as much or as little toilet paper as he or she wants. Take some for yourself, too. Have each person count the number of squares they took. Everyone tells one thing about himself or herself for each square they have taken. For example, if a member takes four squares, they may say: 1. Love dogs 2. Favorite color is blue 3. School is hard 4. I live with my mom. This is also a great assessment tool to see how comfortable clients are to opening up about more concerning issues.

Modality:
How I Role is a great getting to know you and ice breaker activity. It can be used in large or small groups.

Group
School

CHIT CHAT
Theme: Ice Breaker

Material:
*Connect 4

Advance Preparation:
None

Description and Discussion:
Begin by asking client if they have ever played the game Connect 4. For those unfamiliar with the game, quickly go over the rules, and for those who do, tell them that you will play a slightly different version, described as follows.

Decide who will go first. Ask the client if they would like to go first. This may tell you how comfortable they feel. The client is trying to get four in a row vertically, horizontally, or diagonally. The Chit Chat version is different because each time a person has a turn, he or she tells something about him or herself or asks the other player a question.

Since most people find Connect 4 enjoyable, this game can be a fun getting to know you tool.

Modality:
Chit Chat can be used wherever the leader feels comfortable overseeing the activity.

Individual
Couples
Sibling

Connect 4 is a trademark of Hasbro. All rights reserved. Used with permission.

LET'S CONNECT
Theme: Assessments

Material:
* Connect 4
* Timer

Advance Preparation:
Copy each question from the Connect Four Assessment sheet. Cut questions and put them into a bowl so that the client can pull out the question randomly. If you are working with couples, the clients may have questions of their own to use instead. It is helpful to copy questions on card stock and laminate them if you plan on using the game over again.

Description and Discussion:
Begin by asking client if they have ever played Connect 4. For those unfamiliar with the game, quickly go over the rules, and for those who do know it, tell them that you will play a different version, described as follows.

Decide who will go first. Ask the client if they would like to go first. This indicates how comfortable they feel. The client is trying to get four in a row vertically, horizontally, or diagonally. Each time a person takes a turn they will draw a question from the stockpile of questions, though they will only have two minutes (or however long the session allows) to answer.

After playing the game as an Ice Breaker, it will be easy to use the game as an assessment tool in the future. Be sure to use the timer, so possible past arguments do not become part of the session.

Modality:
This activity is better used in professional offices where the assessment can be appropriately monitored and boundaries can be mediated.

Individual
Couples
Sibling
Ice Breaker
Self- Esteem

SELF- ESTEEM ASSESSMENT QUESTIONS

If you could change one thing about yourself, what would it be?	What is one thing you are good at?
What makes you happy?	When is the last time you laughed?
What is unique about you?	What is your favorite part of your body?
What is your least favorite part of your body?	Tell me about a problem you are having.
Finish this sentence My parents think…	Tell me what people think about you at school.

COUPLES ASSESSMENT QUESTIONS

What is your favorite memory with your spouse?	What would you like to change about your relationship with your spouse?
What do you fight about the most?	What is your favorite thing to do with your spouse?
If you could change one thing about your spouse, what would you change?	If your spouse changed one thing about you, what would they change?
What do you laugh about most when you are together?	Tell me a time you felt happy when you were with your spouse.
Tell me a time you felt sad or angry.	Tell me a special memory of you and your spouse.

SECTION TWO:

Feelings
Self-Esteem
Social Skills

WHAT I LIKE ABOUT ME
Theme: Self- Esteem

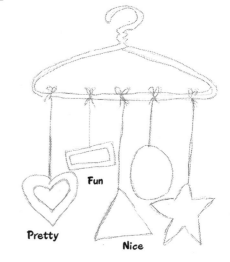

Material:
* Wire Hanger
* Safety Scissors
* String
* Construction Paper
* Glue
* Paint, Crayons, or Markers
* Pretties: such as sparklers

Advance Preparation:
Cover area with newspaper, cut out a few shapes, and poke hole in top of each shape. Put string through shape.

Description and Discussion:
This project provides opportunities to openly communicate while building a mobile and self-esteem.

Self-esteem adds value to how we feel about ourselves. As our self-value rises, other factors in our life improve, such as grades, relationships, and self worth.

Modality:
This project is a favorite in a group or school setting. When used in these settings, it is better to have member write positive remarks about each of their group members on the shapes before trading them. After they have traded the shapes, they hang the shapes and string from the hanger to create a mobile.

For individuals, the client can describe things they like about themselves or things they are good at.

Group
Sibling
Individual
School
Team Work

SPECIAL ME
Theme: Self- Esteem

Material:
* Markers
* Construction Paper
* Safety Scissors
* Glue
* Tape
* Aluminum Foil if wanted
* Gems if wanted

Advance Preparation:
1. Use scissors to a cut band of construction paper 18 inches. Measure the length to fit around head; then cut a zigzag shape into top of the band, so the end result is a crown.
2. Use markers to color the crown.
3. Cut pieces of foil in gem shapes and glue them onto crown.
4. Overlap the ends and tape them together.
5. Cut pieces of shapes to write comments about self or each other to increase self-esteem.
6. Glue shapes with positive comments onto crown.

Description and Discussion:
This project gives opportunity to build a self-esteem crown while developing communication and the counseling relationship.

Self-esteem is important because it adds value to how we feel about others or ourselves. As our self-value increases, other factors in our life improve, such as grades, relationships, and, of course, self worth.

Modality:
This project can be used with individuals or groups, though kids seem to love the group experience and sharing their charms for their crowns. When used in a group setting, have each member go around and write positive remarks about their group members and trade shapes.

For individuals, the client can describe things they like about themselves or things they are good at.

Group	School	Individual
Sibling	Team Work	

FACE YOUR FEELINGS
Theme: Feelings

Material:
* Wooden Spoons or Small Paper Plates
* Markers
* Glue
* Fabric
* If using Plate puppets, you'll need Popsicle sticks.

Advance Preparation:
Cover area with newspaper.
Option to paint wooden spoon or plate skin tone
Use markers to draw faces of various feelings
Glue yarn onto back and top of spoon or plate for hair
Can glue fabric onto spoon handle for costume.

For Popsicle plate puppets: Glue plate with various feeling faces onto Popsicle.

Description and Discussion:
It is hard for some to discuss feelings, especially feelings that have been covered for some time. This creative activity is beneficial because it includes the use of wooden spoons or Popsicle puppets to act out feelings or scenarios.

Children's artwork is therapeutic in session and is helpful to guide the client into opening up his or her feelings. Have the client build puppets representing happy, sad, mad, frustrated, scared, and other feelings they may have. Discuss these feelings as they are being built. This activity may take more than one session.

Modality:
This activity can become personal and is best used in individual sessions by a trained, sensitive caregiver.

Individual

FEELINGS SCENERIOS
Theme: Feelings

Material:
* Wooden Spoon Puppet or Popsicle Puppet from previous Face Your Feelings Activity

Advance Preparation:
Copy each scenario from the Puppet Scenario Sheet. Cut the scenarios out and put them into a bowl. Then have the client pull out scenarios objectively. It is helpful to copy the scenarios on card stock and laminate if you plan on using over again.

Description and Discussion:
It is hard to discuss feelings, especially feelings that have been covered for some time. This activity is creative and is a way to use play therapy and scenarios with the wooden spoons or Popsicle puppets after being made.

Use the puppets from the previous activity to role-play scenarios from attached sheet. If other themes arise, stop or make note to talk about those topics in a later session. This can be used as a form of assessment as well.

Modality:
This activity can become personal and is best used in individual sessions by a trained sensitive caregiver.

Individual

PUPPET SCENERIO SHEET

Kids at lunch won't let you sit at their table. Act this out.	Kids at recess won't let you play with them. What do you do?
A boy in your class cuts in front of you when lining up.	Your teacher calls your name for talking out loud when it wasn't you. How does this make you feel?
Your mom says she will talk to you later, but she spends most of her time on the cell phone.	You want to spend alone time with dad, but his new girlfriend is always over.
You want a new toy or game. How do you go about getting it?	You want to stay up late, but your parents want you to go to bed. What do you do?
I feel …	When I am with my brother or sister I feel.

FINDERS KEEPERS
Theme: Feelings

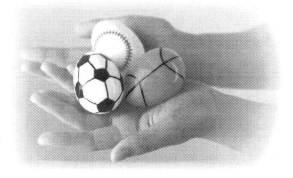

Materials:
* Plastic eggs

Advance Preparation:
Cut out and fill eggs with scenarios or feelings
Hide eggs

Description and Discussion:
First decide if you are playing to be aware of feelings or scenarios. Both options are attached.
If the purpose of playing is to gain more awareness of feelings, take some time to discuss the
differences between feeling words. For example, angry and sad sometimes feel the same, but
are very different. Your body may feel uncomfortable. The body is tense and it is hard to
concentrate.

Next, explain that there are a certain number of eggs hidden and they are to go find them.
Depending on how you are playing the game, when an egg is found the participants can act
out their usual response to the scenario or describe a time when they felt the feeling. Then
have them tell a trigger for this feeling, such as tense body and how to better cope with
the trigger before it escalates. The leader can reward the members with candy for thinking
through their answers. This will encourage them to do the same thinking in the following
scenarios and feelings. They play until all eggs are found. At the end you can give reward
(attached).

Modality
This activity can facilitate identification and expression of feelings and therefore should be
used in a private atmosphere or in a small group setting.

Group
Siblings
Individual

FEELING CARDS

Happy	Sad
Mad	Scared
Anxious	Annoyed/ Frustrated

SCENERIOS

John took your pencil when you weren't looking, and you didn't have it when it was quiz time.	Your sibling left you a note saying they love you.
You walked in when your mom and dad were fighting.	Extra:
All your friends get to go to a birthday party except you. How do you feel?	Extra:

PIECE TOGETHER
Theme: Feelings, Extended Session Material

Materials:
* Empty cereal box

Advance Preparation:
Cut the front portion of cereal box into a square. On the back of the square, where there are no markings, draw puzzle piece shapes. In each puzzle piece write questions that need to be asked or confronted during the counseling session. The client can write in a few questions if they would like to, as well. If the client does not come up with questions, the leader should write all the questions. Cut out the pieces of the puzzle. When putting pieces back together, answer the prepared questions. The client may chose to tape the puzzle together or leave it apart for future playing.

Option I: Prepare by writing feelings or social skills on back of the puzzle pieces. When putting the puzzle together, discuss the word or words on back.

Modality:
This activity can become sensitive; therefore it is best used in a private, individual environment. The leader should be cautious not to interpret answers incorrectly.

Individual

Sample questions:

1. What is your favorite hobby?
2. If you could change one thing about your life what would it be?
3. What are some things that make you angry?
4. What makes you laugh out loud?
5. What is your favorite toy?
6. Who is your favorite friend?
7. When is the last time you had an argument with your mom/dad?
8. What do you do when you feel sad?
9. Do you have pets?
10. Have you ever been in trouble at school? Tell me about it.

Feelings can be found in the back section of this book titled Resource. Use the list of feelings if you choose to use game idea II. Some more common feelings are mad, sad, nervous, scared, and hyper.

PIECE TOGETHER CONTINUED
Theme: Feelings, Further Session Material

Sample Scenarios:

1. Dad was supposed to pick you up at 6:00 P.M. and it is 6:20. He still hasn't come to pick you up. How do you feel, and what do you think is best to handle this situation?

2. A friend at school borrowed your favorite shirt when she spent the night, and now she says she cannot find it. What should you do?

3. Your dog looks sick. He is getting old. How does this feel and what can you do to feel better?

4. Your brother always walks in your room without knocking. He is so annoying. What can you do?

5. You usually make good grades, but lately you just can't concentrate. What is going on? Should you just try to pull your grades up or should you talk to someone?

6. Your parents always ask you to call the other parent. Can't they just do it themselves? Should you talk to them about it or just do as you are told?

7. All your friends are playing outside, and, as much as you want to join them, there is one mean bully in the crowd. Do you go or just play alone inside?

8. Tell about a time you had to stand up for a friend.

9. Tell about a time you felt you where mistreated.

10. Tell about a time you where given the benefit of the doubt.

HUNT
Theme: Social-Skills

Materials:
* Make picture clues or print out clip art clues

      Picture clue ideas: Mailbox, pillow, lamp, and water hose.

      Verbal clue ideas: Hop to where you rest your head at night

        Tip Toe to what you would use if you wanted to water the grass

      Therapeutic Ideas: Go find one thing you could hit and not get in trouble. If you punch me 8 times you feel better, and you also feel better when you rest your head on me too.

Advance Preparation:
Place either pictures or clues in hidden spots

Description and Discussion:
This is a game to build friendships and social skills while going on a scavenger hunt to find picture clues. Picture clues have previously been hidden throughout the house or office. Give the client or team the first picture clue to start the hunt. They will play until they come to the end of the hunt where everyone will discuss social skills used.

Modality:
This game fits any case where you are trying to bond or build social skills or self-esteem.

Group
Individual
Siblings
Family

FUN AND FIND
Theme: Social skills

Materials:
* Clip art or drawings client has completed
* Postcards or cut paper

Advance Preparation:
None

Description and Discussion:
Explain to client that taking a break from heated situations allows time to calm down and think.

Print or draw fun but comforting icons that can be found at home or in counseling sessions to practice activity. Cut out pictures and paste them on small cards (index cards) so they will last longer. Shuffle pictures then put them in a container. When the card is drawn, go together to find the item in the picture. You can discuss why you drew that picture in home or office or even outside. Set a timer to see how fast you can find it.

If playing in groups, have them work together or make it a challenge. This activity can teach the leader about clients via their discussion of the pictures. This activity is fun, simple, and effortlessly builds on the relationship of the ones participating.

Modality:
Fun and Find enhances problem-solving skills and coping strategies. The activity can take up to an hour to complete, therefore is best used with smaller groups where the activity does not run as long.

Individual
Group
Sibling

GOOD OR NOT SO GOOD
Theme: Social Skills

Materials:
* None

Advance Preparation:
None

Description and Discussion:
This activity can be used for many purposes, though it will be described using social skills in groups and school environments. The leader can start first to demonstrate. The leader gives examples of good and bad social skills. If the action is a good or positive one, such as hugging, the group claps once. If the action is negative, say hitting, they would clap twice. Encourage group members to add more negative and positive social skills to the mix.

This activity can be a good assessment tool. The client's input can inform a counselor as to what is going on in his or her life.

Example positive actions:
Eye contact
Saying please and thank you
Making friends
Speaking in a reasonable tone of voice
Helping others
Sharing

Example negative actions:
Example
Hitting
Shouting
Pushing
Not sharing
Threatening

Modality:
Although this activity may seem fit for a younger crowd, it can be used for various ages.

Group
School

SECTION THREE:

Communication
Team Work
Habits

I CAN DO THAT
Theme: Communication and Social Skills

Materials:
* Blocks

Advance Preparation:
None

Description and Discussion:
You will need two sets of the same blocks or four sets if you are working with a group. It takes a bit of memory and sense of humor for this activity. If the client becomes frustrated easily, this will work on how to handle those feelings appropriately.

Set the blocks in two separate areas where they cannot be seen. Have a leader set up one set of the blocks or look at how you have set them up. The leader then goes back to his or her group and communicates how to build the blocks. Group members can take turns being the communicator / leader. The communicator / leader cannot touch the blocks when reporting back to group members. The leader may become frustrated due to not being hands on. Group members may get overwhelmed with having to relay on communication. Facilitate feelings that may arise before becoming out of hand and use these as teaching tools to quicken time and enhance group's overall effectiveness. Try activity 2 or 3 times to build on skill and time.

Discuss how members felt about activity. Was it easier being a member or communicator? Did any of the members notice triggers of frustration or aggravation and how did they cope with it?

Modality:
This activity strengthens impulse control, communication, and self-regulation. It should be used where there is enough room to set up two sets of blocks.

Group
Sibling

GROUP HOOP
Theme: Communication

Materials:
* Round large object such as a Hula-Hoop or large rope tied

Advance Preparation:
None

Description and Discussion:
Begin by having a discussion about communication. Discuss manners and positive and negative communication. Using manners are polite, for instance saying please and thank you.

What are various ways we all communicate others?
Voice
Hands
Expressions
Feelings
Drawings
Tools: Computers, phones, drawing pads

Positive and Negative Communication:
Give the example:

If your best friend was running a marathon and you were their coach, what communication would you use?

Open the floor to suggestions and you may add the following: Great job; Faster; Pick up your feet; You're doing awesome, etc.

Next, talk about negative communication and give examples such as: You're not fast enough; You can't run, etc.

How would the two different communication styles make the marathon runner feel?

Activity:
Begin by standing in circle holding hands. Have the hula-hoop on the arms of two group members and have members move the hula-hoop along the circle when the timer starts until it gets back to the initial person. Move the hula hoop or rope by stepping through it or putting your head through the circle. Just move as quickly as possible to get the hoop from your body to the next person's body without letting go of the next person's hand. Repeat game to beat previous timed game. Also, applaud the positive communication given during the game. Stop between tries to give members a chance to discuss positive and negative communication and social skills.

GROUP HOOP CONTINUED
Theme: Communication

Modality:
This is an excellent team building game that encourages communication. Activity requires a lot of room.

Group
Sibling
Families
School Groups

Guardian of Pennington Girls signed release for picture in book.

WALK THIS WAY
Theme: Communication

Materials:
* Communication Walkers

Advance Preparation:
Either buy or make communication walkers

To Make Walkers: Take two pieces of wood about 4 feet in length and 4 inches in width. Place two ropes with handles or knots at the end for holding towards the front and middle of each walker. You will need 4 total handle ropes.

Description and Discussion:
Working together, keeping up good friendships, and maintaining a healthy relationship takes patience and communication. Have the client or counselor talk about positive and negative communication. Assist the clients to get on walkers, one as the leader and one as the communicator; then trade roles. Try to walk to a marked destination, make turn, and come back to initial spot. To make activity more challenging, have listener or the person on the back closes their eyes.

After everyone has had a chance to lead walkers, discuss what positive and negative communication took place. Was the activity more challenging than expected?

Modality:
This activity builds relationships. It can strengthen social, communication, and group skills.

Individually
Group
Sibling

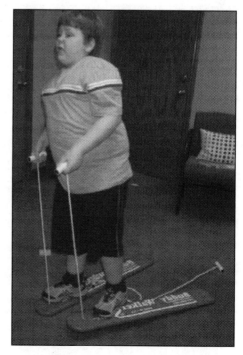

Guardian of H.W signed release.

GUESS WHAT
Theme: Communication

Materials:
*Various animal stickers

Advance Preparation:
None

Description and Discussion:
Discuss the importance of communication and sense of humor. Have a talk about the different ways we communicate. Encourage the members to use different means of communication. Speak about social skills: taking turns, talking softly and politely, sharing, being patience, and kind.

Pick the client using the best social skills to have a turn first. This will be a flag for the others members to be more aware of their own skills. The chosen person turns their back to the group as the leader/counselor places a sticker on their back. The person can then face the group.

The other members practice using communication to describe the animal. Keep playing until everyone gets a turn. Have members point out positive social skills used.

Modality:
I liked using this in guidance classroom settings, but I have also used it in the home and in the office.

Group
School Counseling

MEET IN THE MIDDLE
Theme: Team Work

Materials:
*String
*Space for obstacle
*Obstacle course
*Reward

Advance Preparation:
Run string through obstacle

Description and Discussion:
If working with an individual this is a good exercise to build a counseling relationship. If working with siblings or two group members this is a team game and should be fun for all.

Have each member start on opposite ends of the string. Ask the participants to go through obstacles until they meet. Use encouraging words such as: good job and thanks. Give positive feedback as activity is played.

Modality:
This is a great activity to work out bullying, team differences, sibling rivalry, family dynamics, and it encourages cooperation. This game is fun when played as a group. It is also rewarding when played individually with your client to build on the counselor/client relationship, client's self-esteem, and social skills. If it is possible to go to the client's home, it can be an exciting exercise to try in his or her home environment.

Individual
Sibling
Group
Family
Teams

PYRAMID
Theme: Team Work

Materials:
*6 small cups
*1 rubber band
*2 strings for every player tied to the rubber band

Advance Preparation:
Tie two strings to the one rubber band for each player. Place cups rim side down on platform or floor.

Description and Discussion:
What are social skills?
Being polite
Saying Please
Saying Thank you
Waiting your Turn
Being Patient
Being Calm

Discuss the importance of using social skills and manners.

Describe how each member will be given two strings that are attached to a rubber band. The group or client and counselor are to use strings to maneuver rubber band around cups without touching the cups with their hands. Once the rubber band is around the cup, begin stacking the cups in a pyramid. If a cup falls, use the string or rubber band to stand it right side up. This activity can test one's patience and is a good test of social skills and builds teamwork.

Modality:
This is a great icebreaker activity, but can also be used to assess strength and weakness in teams. I use it in counseling to discuss social skills and time the activity to build on strengths.

Individual
Group
Sibling
Family

ONE LOG AT A TIME
Theme: Team Work

Materials:
* Fake logs: Laminated brown construction paper

Advance Preparation:
None

Description and Discussion:
Prepare group members by letting them know this activity may take practice. Have the group picture a scenario where they are on one side of a lake and there is a pack of wild wolves coming. All members need to get across quickly and safely. The leader must use logs to get across, but explain if he or she puts a log down without having a foot on the log, it will float away. Also, it is important for the last member to pick up the logs as they cross so the wolves cannot follow. Remind group to always have one foot on a log so that it will not float away. The last member picks up logs as they cross to keep wolves from crossing.

Modality:
This is a great activity to bring about team cohesiveness. The activity works well with specific groups such as girls only, Boy Scouts, families, or siblings.

Group
School
Sibling
Family

This is not an original activity. I would love to give credit to the originator of this activity, but I am not sure where it originated. I first heard it at a Project Adventure Training and have been using it ever since. Please note that it is borrowed to help others and not stolen.

GROW AWAY THOSE NASTY OL' HABITS
Theme: Habits New and Old

Materials:
> Planting Materials
> > *Plants or seeds
> > *Gloves if wanted
> > *Something to dig with
> > *Newspaper
> > *Colors or marker

Advance Preparation:

Have clients write on the newspaper any habits they want to get rid of. For example: hitting, kicking, talking back, and others that are of concern. Ask client to write or draw as much or as little as they want on newspaper (biodegradable) about their concerns and the issues they have caused. There are no boundaries. After the newspaper is prepared, have the client fold or crumple the pieces to fit into the ground.

Description and Discussion:

Take newspaper and client to a chosen sight. Dig a hole and place newspaper in it. Comment that we have taken these feelings and now we are going to grow new, more healthful feelings. This will be a special place for client to come as much or little as needed. Have client plant flower, cover with dirt, and water if needed. Encourage the client to use chosen place as a safe spot to visit when future feelings arise.

Modality:

This activity can become very emotional and should be used in individual or family environments that are safe and comfortable.

Individually
Family

MARBLES OR QUARTERS
Theme: Bringing out the best!

Materials:
* Any type of small visual objects such as: marble, quarters, and stones.
* Container

Advance Preparation:
Discuss two to three things client would like to have or work towards (new game, go to eat at Chuck E. Cheese, to upgrade their cell phone, be allowed to have a few friends spend the night.)

If working on this game as a family, think of things the family would enjoy doing together. For instance, when working with teenagers and their moms, they may have the rewards such as: getting a manicure together, renting a movie and having a movie night, going to the zoo.)

Remember, rewards have to be worthy for activity to work. On the other end, the discipline system must also be in place. Discipline plans will be discussed later.

Next prepare a cup or clear container to collect the marbles in. Mark three reward lines on the cup. The first line ¼ of the way up, the second line ½, the third line ¾ up, and the rim will be reaching the main goal and reward.

This activity should be conformed to fit the family. If a child needs to reach the line faster for their self-esteem, a cup with 4 total limits is better. An older child may only need two reward lines. The number of marbles or quarters does not matter as much as meeting the reward line. Now that the rewards have been decided and the container is ready, lets discuss the activity in depth.

Description and Discussion:
This activity can be used for many reasons: to gain awareness of parent relationship, to reward positive behavior in a child, to rid negative behavior by noticing more positive behaviors, to become a closer family unit. Basically, if you are using this activity as a tool to stop arguing between siblings, then when you notice good companionship, social skills, and manners you would reward a marble. Soon the positive behavior will increase and negative behaviors will decrease.

Example tasks to be rewarded:
Have your child do something the first time a parent asks.
Improve grades
Put up laundry

The most important thing is for the goals to be what the child needs to improve on, their biggest challenges.

MARBLES OR QUARTERS CONTINUED
Theme: Bringing out the best!

For parents:
Knock on door before entering
Say please and thank you
Give the child some space

These are only a few examples. Goals should come from the family or individual.

When a goal is accomplished, a marble or quarter is rewarded. It is exciting to watch the families have fun with this activity instead of using the old yelling technique, or becoming frustrated and overwhelmed.

Modality:
This can be implemented in classrooms, Girl or Boy Scouts, sales meetings, and counseling groups as long as it is adjusted to be age appropriate.

Group
Individual
Family
Sibling

SECTION FOUR:

Grief
Discipline
Rewards
Resources

GROW AWAY GRIEF
Theme: Grief

Materials:
> Planting Materials
>> *Plants or seeds
>> *Gloves (optional)
>> *A tool for digging
>> *Newspaper
>> *Colors or marker

Advance Preparation:
Set aside time where leader and client can discuss grief issues. Explain how this is a special moment and activity just for the person or pet they are grieving for. Explain how they will write and draw about their feelings on newspaper since it is biodegradable. After they prepare their newspaper, they tear it into small pieces.

Description and Discussion:
Take the shredded newspaper and the client to a chosen sight. Dig a hole and place newspaper in it. Discuss getting rid of negative feelings and growing new, more healthful feelings. This will be a special place for the client to come as much or little as needed. Have them place the plant, cover it with dirt, and encourage them when future feelings arise to choose healthy alternatives to grieve such as crying, reading a poem, or talking.

Modality:
This activity can become emotional and should be used in individual or family environments that are safe and comfortable.

Individually
Family

DISCIPLINE MADE EASY
Theme: Discipline

Materials:
*Kids' favorite things
*Parent's dedication and consistency
*Markers and Paper

Advance Preparation:
Always have reward / marble system in place

Description and Discussion:
Rewarding positive behaviors will result in fewer negative behaviors. For instance, if a child is cursing, give a marble for noticing polite, well-mannered communication. Parents will soon notice better mannered vocabulary.

Child's discipline needs to be written and visible. If rules are made by child and agreed on by family, plan tends to be more successful. It is never too late to implement discipline.

Objects important to kids:
Computer
Cell Phone
Friends
Hanging out
Freedom
Video Games

If you discipline by taking away insignificant objects, it will not work.

Sit the family down and ask everyone's opinion on the top three concerns. For instance they may be:
Staying on the phone too late
Locking the door
Not doing as told
Being disrespectful

Only pick the top three concerns. Although children and adults should discuss rules and expectations, the adults should have the final say, as they are the ones responsible for implementing the discipline plan. Define rules very clearly to prevent later misunderstanding. The discipline system can be tweaked, though, once made to fit the family, it should not be negotiated or compromised, as this will lead to future complaints from child.

Modality:
Kids like to have control of their lives and strive to do better when they are given a challenge. Having kids come up with their own discipline system almost always secures success. This discipline system works for all grades and ages. For younger children, such as pre-kindergarteners, time outs have proven to be effective if implemented and used correctly.

Individual

SAFETY SACK:

Have fun putting together a safety sack for a client or your own children. The items in the sack are to be used when feeling frustrated, sad, lonely, or other numerous feelings. The items are meant to replace unhealthy impulse reactions.

Safety Sack Items

1. Piece of Chewing gum
2. Journal and Pen
3. Paper and Crayons
4. Puzzle
5. Birthday Blower
   -Blow when you feel angry
6. Cotton Balls
   -Blow across room
7. Lil' deck of cards
8. Playdough or Putty
9. Stuffed animal
10. Homemade postcard for communication

A few words...

I hope you enjoyed the book and found the activities helpful. If you have any questions or would like to keep updated on further activities, log onto www.ambercounselor.com or e-mail Amber Kuntz, LPC at www.ambercounselor@gmail.com.

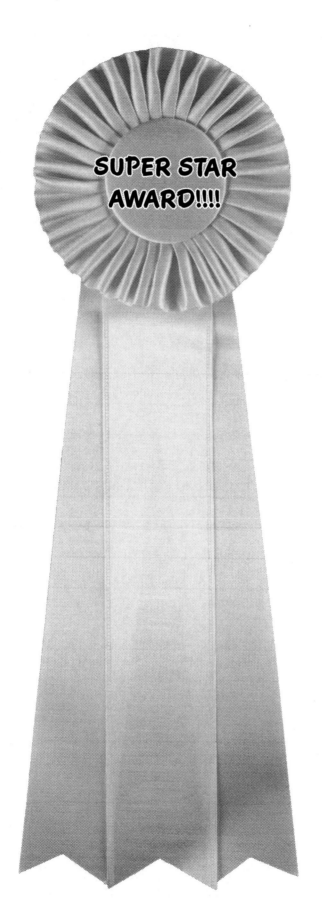

FEELING WORDS

Angry
Anxious
Bored
Confident
Confused
Curious
Depressed
Determined
Embarrassed
Excited
Fearful
Frightened
Frustrated
Guilty
Happy
Helpless
Hopeful
Hurt
Innocent
Interested
Jealous
Lonely
Loved
Miserable
Negative
Paranoid
Peaceful
Proud
Regretful
Relieved
Sad
Satisfied
Shocked
Shy
Sorry
Stubborn
Sure
Surprised
Thoughtful
Undecided
Withdrawn

Resources

Grief
1. A Keepsake to Commerorate the Loss of a Loved One, Marianne Richmond
1. Healing Children's Grief, GH Christ
2. Healing the Bereaved Child, AD Wolfelt
3. Tear Soup, Pat Schweibert

Preparing for Divorce or Separation Books:
1. *Difficult Questions Kids Ask and Are Too Afraid To Ask About Divorce*, Meg F Shneid
2. *Co-Parenting After Divorce is Hard,* Philip Michael Stahl
3. *How to Talk to Your Child About Divorce,* Jill Soderman
4. *Making Divorce Easier on Your Child,* Nicholas Long

Books For Kids:
1. Two Homes, Claire Masural
2. Dinosaurs Divorce, Marc Brown
3. Mama and Daddy Bears Divorce, Cornelia Maude Spelman
4. My Family's Changing, Pat Thomas
5. I Don't Want to Talk About It, Jeanie Franz Ransom
6. Was it the Chocolate Pudding?, Sandra Livings
7. It's Not Your Fault KoKo Bear, Vicki Lansky

Feelings:
1. It's Okay To Be Different, Todd Parr
2. The Way I Feel by Janan Cain
3. I'm Gonna Like Me: Letting Off a Little Self-Esteem, Jamie Lee Curtis
4. The Feelings Book: The Care & Keeping of Your Emotions, Dr Lynda Madison, Ph.D., Lynda Madison in Books
5. A Smart Girl's Guide to Friendship Troubles (American Girl Library)Angela Martini, Patti Kelley Crisswell
6. A Smart Girl's Guide to Sticky SituationsNancy Holyoke, Norm Bendell, Norm Bendell
7. The Care and Keeping of Me: The Body Book Journal Pleasant Company Publications, Norm Bendell

Great Websites
http://www.keepkidshealthy.com/
http://kidshealth.org
http://www.webmd.com/mental-health/default.htm
www.ambercounselor.com

In this book, Amber Kuntz has compiled a gathering of activities from practitioners, clients, and original material. Techniques are outlined for relationship building, teamwork, and treating kids of all ages and their families. The above resources are merely offered as sources of information and are not affiliated with Amber Kuntz, LPC or Business.

Journal Pages

Journal Pages

Journal Pages

Journal Pages

Journal Pages